Announcements
from the
Planetarium

Announcements from the Planetarium

Judith Arcana

FLOWSTONE PRESS
Illinois Valley, Oregon

Sometimes I think life is just a rodeo –
the trick is to ride, and make it to the bell.

- John Fogerty

FLOWSTONE PRESS

Announcements from the Planetarium
Copyright © 2017 Judith Arcana

ISBN 978-1-945824-07-4

Front cover image by Jeremy Thomas, courtesy unsplash

Back cover image by Greg Rakozy, courtesy unsplash

Author photo by Lynda Koolish

Layout and cover design by Ryan Forsythe

First Flowstone Press Edition,
April 2017

Contents

Contents

Announcements from the Planetarium

ONE

as the sweetapple reddens on a high branch
   high on the highest branch and the applepickers forgot –
no, not forgot: were unable to reach.

- Sappho
(as translated by Anne Carson)

Zombies on Skateboards

We met in the center of the city
near a captive tree in the plaza
a tree locked in a circle of iron
bars with sharp points. He was
growling, shouting, loud: *People!*
Give us your change! He was one
of a pack, white kids with dreads
dressed in grimy surplus khaki
holding confused dogs on leashes.

Those kids were tattooed, with art
that looked like money. He reached
for my phoenix-in-flames, held my arm
next to his zombies-on-skateboards.
I said, *Good name for a band.*
He laughed, looking into my eyes.
We were inside each other's eyes.
He said, *I bet you can remember*
the day the sun was born, Granma.

The first true thing

You're sad to leave the first true thing
the first true thing you know won't stay
it runs like water all down your life
rushes hot behind your heart
slides inside like dreams talking
deep whispers in your mind will go
on telling that true thing.

That true thing will go down rocks
into ground, on past deep winter
gone, but you can know it, you can
remember; use it to learn language
for listening, for seeing things
when they're really there, yes
and when they're not.

A different thing

I'm not saying I'm done collecting knowledge.
I won't stop picking up shiny bits of information.
I'm saying *wisdom* is a different thing – it's not
about collection, accumulation. Maybe it's like
sorting, arranging, mixing and then – steeping.
Like making tea: letting it steep, letting it sit
a while, sometimes tasting it, learning what it is
after you wait through the time it's been steeping.

Fact is, everybody's wise sometimes, babies
even, high school sophomores, thirty-seven
year old bank managers. But as the main thing
the main way of the mind, the way that comes
later – *wisdom* is, or means, something else.
Something babies, high school sophomores
and thirty-seven year old bank managers don't
do, have or use. You can be this old and not be
wise, but you can't be wise if you're not this old.
Not this much, this long, this often. Not as a habit.

The gift comes late, perhaps as compensation.

Speculative Music Theory:
   Like Dancing About Architecture #1

Was your own first music simple
lullabye hushabye humming?
Or was it your grandpa's broken
muttering of the American words
to "Happy Birthday," while cousins
who'd been here years before him
sang it like they'd been here always
even though they hadn't? You –
you're the one who was born here.

Dreaming the Indian Ocean

You old ones, my people, when you passed childhood
were you surprised to learn so many had the same dream?
Had you thought, like me, you were the only small one
who turned your bed to a boat in the clear deep water
a boat in deep blue sky, sailing and flying the world?
Did you get where you wanted to go? Where was that?

I wanted to fly in my bed all the way to the Indian Ocean
where the great whales of every sea would swim green
deep water each year, giving birth and nursing their young.
What made that my dream? What could I have known, then
of their lives? This is the mystery left from my youth, deep
in the time before knowledge. The rest, now, I understand.

1956

The year I started high school Babe Didrikson died.
Before I knew there was more to know, I saw women
ministering to children, to men. Grace Kelly married
the Prince of Monaco in a special on TV. *Life*
magazine said the "most spectacular success"
for American women was "having babies."
Clairol started asking: Does she or doesn't she?
Marilyn Monroe & Kim Novak were big stars.
Peyton Place was hot; so was *The Nun's Story*.

Presbyterians ordained their first woman minister
in Syracuse, while Golda Myerson from Milwaukee
(a woman my Aunt Bella claimed to know)
changed her name to Meir to be a prime minister.
I'd no idea what might come of all that ministration –
what would happen next, what would be good, bad
and not. I was thirteen years old, listening to Little
Richard rip it up. The word sounded like menstruation –
which had to be way more important. I did know that.

You may have heard about my situation

We don't know how it happened: I started
growing, couldn't stop, couldn't stop, couldn't
even though I wanted to. Even though I wanted
to stop, I grew right out of all my clothes, grew
out of my clothes and stopped trying to get new
ones. I stopped trying to get new ones and stayed
in the house. I stayed in the house and watched TV.

I watched TV on the living room sofa; I couldn't
fit into the chairs, even Poppa's La-Z-Boy rocker.
Even Poppa's La-Z-Boy rocker got too small.
If I bent my elbows, they touched both arms
of the sofa when I sat square in the middle.
I sat square in the middle of the sofa every day
watching whatever was on TV, even though it flipped.

I sat still, trying to hush my body, hoping to
stop. But it kept on and pretty soon my hips
touched the sofa's arms when I centered myself.
My head was not far from the ceiling and oh!
people, the sofa frame started to creak! It creaked
so loud I could not hear what news anchors said
to the camera, their faces sometimes flipping.

I could not hear the hyenas, snuffling like always
over the zebra carcass on the Discovery channel.
The Discovery channel called me; they wanted
to do a feature on what they called my *situation*.
How did they hear about me? I still don't know.
What they called my *situation* was serious.
Think about it, people. Try to imagine this:

I could hardly squeeze through the hallways
upstairs or down, even sideways and stooping.
Sideways and stooping, I pushed out late one night
when there was no moon; there was no moon and I
had no clothes, just an old red tablecloth pulled
off the dining room table. Oh, I wrapped that red
cloth all around me, walked right out into the woods.

My stride was long, my tracks were deep, and
standing straight up, I saw way past our rooftop.
People, I can tell you this: there's nothing up there –
no bird's nest, no lost kite. No tangled balloon string
is causing that flip. Not even branches nearby, twigs
maybe, brushing the roof. I'm as puzzled as you are.
Really. There's no explanation for that, either.

Speculative Music Theory:
Like Dancing About Architecture #3

The music teacher walks along the rows
head down, listening to the voices.
Children are singing the national anthem.
After *home of the brave*, she stands
at the front of the room, calls out
names – yours is one of them – saying
For the pageant, these students will not
sing. These students will move their lips
silently. You are so young when this happens
you don't understand how awful it is.
You accept it, as you accept fire drills.

Then, after years of saying, *Oh no*
I can't sing, you forget yourself in a van
on a road trip – you belt it out with the others.
Then, someone who has no reason
to flatter or protect you says
You have a such a strong voice!
You choose the next song!
Then your heart, behind its seat belt
remembers, and stops for a moment.

Nickel Heart

Everybody knows if you put a nickel on the tracks
before the 5:40 comes through, that nickel turns up
a perfect heart, polished flat and smooth.

Everybody wonders how the nickel stays on the track
why it doesn't slip away from that first touch
of the speeding wheels to its silver body.

Some think a penny will work, but that's not true;
my brother says a penny can bend, don't try it, a penny
folks say, won't do; after all, it's not a nickel.

And who could argue that? So when you got one
you'd cross the big road to the switch yard
and walk the railbed out of town about a mile.

You'd follow that track the long way out of town
way out there where the train would still be coming
pumping like blood straight into your heart.

You need to take your nickel way out of town
out there where the streets turn into highways
sidewalks loosen first to gravel, then to grain.

Right there is where the engineer will brake, where
tracks splice town to field; the train'll slow down –
past there you can't make a heart.

You set your nickel and stand away, loving the sound
of the train in the distance, loving the 5:40 running
fast, on up the rails to make your perfect heart.

Fullerton

This poem is when my son is a baby, nursing a lot
and we're mostly past the hard part, he's eating
applesauce, mashed bananas, oatmeal, gummy bits
of grownup food along with all this milk, so I go out
don't remember why, tell his father *back soon*
or *couple hours* (or what I'm really thinking – no
not that) and go down to the Fullerton bus stop
wearing cut-off blue jeans, white sneakers and a red
t-shirt that says HEY CUBS, THIS IS THE YEAR!

I get whatever it is I've gone for and stand out
at another bus stop carrying packages, paper bags
I have to hold or set down to wait, there's no bus
all the time fills up with thinking (the baby and me
in a small van, driving out far to see the sky)
soon my breasts are aching, dripping, so I go back
to wherever I just came out of, the women's room
fold kleenex over my nipples inside their container
built like a suspension bridge, go back to the corner
step off the curb, look down the street, far down
where there's no bus, no bus, no bus, no sign of a bus
for my paper bags, aching breasts, damp kleenex
I put a thumb out, up at the necessary angle
and the Chrysler appears suddenly, silent, dark blue
or maybe it's even purple and the window slides
down like in a movie and he says *how far you going?*

We're on Lake Shore Drive in rush hour (if I had
that van, this'd still be a battle) sitting here deep in
creamy pale leather, my wet breasts throbbing
like he knows this, he nods toward my chest and says
are they real? he's driving past Oak Street Beach
left hand at ten o'clock, right hand in left breast
pocket slips a small folded case out of his jacket
eases it down between his legs where he opens it
takes out fifty-dollar bills, they are fifties, I look
twice, wondering who's on the fifty as he lays
them down, one at a time, on his thigh, sliding them
down the fabric, spreading the bills along his leg
in a narrow fan, hand steady as he drives the limit
barely moving his eyes, tipping his chin slightly
toward my breasts, his fingers still stroking
the fifties, his thigh, the open case between his legs –

At North Avenue his eyes turn right, to my nipples, rise
to my throat, eyes, fall down to my swollen wet breasts
he licks his lips and says again *how far you going?*
several minutes (hours, days, weeks) go by in three
or four or five seconds as I think about this man sucking
my baby's milk, about his fanned-out fifties, about escaping
from my marriage sooner than later, I think about those
things in less time than it takes you to read these words
before I say, Fullerton – I'm going up to Fullerton.

But actually *(mixtape #3)*

An old woman who knew all
the many ways of the fairy folk
lived alone, far out on the moors.

Among the black cinder cones
of the great volcano Haleakala
there lived a very old woman
with a calabash of magic drink.

They said: Nature is a magic theater.
Our mother is the Magician. She says
to each of her children: Some believe
time changes things, but actually you
will have to change them, yourself.

...... including words from Ethel Johnston Phelps / Helen L. Berkey /
the Upanishads / Andy Warhol

What the birds say

...the birds bring messages from the dead,
and the dead bring messages from the universe. ~ Susan Griffin

That year I lived in Chicago again, back home
by the lake, but getting ready to leave.
I was thinking of the past when they died;
birds came every day, flying me into the future.

I lived with the birds; we nested almost together
up on the third floor corner. They coveted my porch
and my kitchen, flapped into my neighbor's fenced trees.
I envied their sky. I watched their wings.

Winter pigeons huddled at my leaded panes
burbling city secrets in their breasts;
gulls flew seventeen blocks in the spring
to my porch, shrieking *lake, beach,* all over my desk.

The summer birds, sparrows in cherry trees
next door, were louder than light in the morning;
Canada geese came by in the fall, flapping
to Rosehill, walking in grass all over the dead.

Crows fly there round the year, flocking
the graveyard trees. They croak
the raw call of their shiny black throats;
they perch on the gravestones and scream.

No one of mine was there in the ground
but four were dying that year every day
while I walked through Rosehill crying
reading aloud the stones of strangers.

I walked with the birds in Rosehill, listening
thinking of dying, what I would lose and how
it would go for me, after. I waited for messages.
What do they say? I asked each time, *What?*

I asked them all. The raucous gulls laughed at me.
The pigeons said, *We don't care.* The sparrows were
so loud they never heard me and the geese flew south
rising on wings spread like blankets all over my head.

I went to the crows. In the garden of dead people
I cried to them each time: *Where have they gone?*
Tell me. They must have words for me, give me
their words. They want me to know. Tell me.

The crows flicked their little black eyes; they looked at me.
They pecked in the grass and made crackling sounds.
I went home and packed up the dishes, folded
my clothes, and put tape around all of the boxes.

The god of your body

When you walk away from people
to the deep steep gorge
where cold streams fall into mist
over rocks among trees, you meet
a rattlesnake, a red winged hawk;
you're afraid but you take the gift:
raw glory, exaltation; you are
grateful for danger and awe.

When a fierce noon goes dark
as green midnight, wind embodies
air and the gale is a wall of rock
moving, when thunderstorms run
the horizon like wolves, a hurricane
stands like a bear in the sky and tornadoes
roar like cougars, you are thrilled
filled with a fear of greatness.

When the land flickers like skin
on a horse, rocks like the hips of a cow
walking her pasture, when earth
quakes, breaks open between
great lakes and big river, or cracks
that long western edge by the sea –
shocked desire and molten dread
converge in the god of your body.

The sun in Montana

Long ago in another life, a life before this one I'm living
now, I learned the hard way, the way of walking miles
to school, home again when it was late, already dark
shadows purple on the deep snow. That way. I learned
security is only in your head. It has no existence, no
meaning outside of you. Is that the only way to learn?
The hard way? Maybe that's how everybody learns
their lessons, simple as day: the sky is blue, the trees
green, the sun yellow, there's no such thing as security.
It's an idea, something to think, not something to have.

That life happened before we said *context* or *conditions* –
before *the thing itself* became impossible, before Heisenberg
got more popular than the Beatles: we could pretend.
We could ignore that absence, the absolute lack of security
in what is still called innocently ignorantly blithely
unthinkingly: *the real world* – the place where
when I was seventeen, the president lied: a pilot (a man
too old to walk to school with me) shot down for lying
for spying; our country shot down by Russia for cheating
for sneaking, and the president lied. He said *national security.*
One short season that show played all the theaters. The lesson
had to come around again, repeat, review, repeat, remember
like a part in a play, like shooting an American
movie: black and white and color; back and forth in time
reviewing lessons of plot, character, crisis, climax.

In my other life we learned our parts, we said our lines
we acted the husband, the lover, the wife, played out
domestic miniatures of the nation: lying and being discovered.
We acted as if we could know, as if security was something
we could get, like orange juice out of the fridge
like a writ of habeas corpus, like a job when they were plenty
like glittering pebbles scattered across the wooden sill of a mine.

TWO

Oh, you should keep on, no matter how difficult
– unless it kills you.
Then you know you've gone too far.

\- Alice Neel

The Crows

Middle-aged women are flocking to see the crows.
They stand on sidewalks, on lawns, and they stare
at the tops of telephone poles, the highest branches
of trees; they sit on picnic tables in the park, perch
at the fountain's edge to watch the crows walk
slowly through strips of sunlight between trees
their black eyes sharp as scissors, knives, razors
black feathers brightly purpled by the light, satin
green and blue, shocking streaks of sudden red
shining off the blackest backs of crows who never
look at the women, crows who walk, stop, open
wide capes of wing and flex their black stick legs
to enter the air. They rise to fly, calling each other
by name, calling each other's names out of the sky.

Art Appreciation, later

On the wall of the gallery
  at the far end of the room:
a long frame of clean wood
  matching these floorboards.
Mounted in that frame: two
  large squares of silent silk
one bright red, one mild grey.
  Years ago, young, she laughed
out loud at what she thought
  pretentious, even arrogant
but now, here, something's
  changed. Her experience
is meditative, the effect
  directly physical. Her body
softens while she stands there
  facing the squares. She's not
concentrating; she's looking.
  She's just being there, being
with the red, the grey. She sees
  threads, the weave of the silk.
Her eyes are simply aimed, not
  focused. She makes no analysis.
Her shoulders, spine and hips
  are loosening; she wants to
get down on the warm wooden
  floor, wishing that long frame
was on the ceiling, so she could
  lie down on her back, gaze up
at the silks floating above her.

Almost never

A little tray with the check on it
a white plate with fresh orange
slices incongruously accompanied
by peppermints in twisted plastic
and the cookies, folded tightly
around the magic words.

Some are aphorisms:
To the young, one day is long; to the old, one life is short.

Some offer admonition:
Where there is discord, we must learn to give way with grace.

Some provide character analysis:
You secretly resent the good luck of others.

But rarely – almost never – do they tell your fortune
the way you need it told (bad news or good
surprise or confirmation), the way you long for
when you break open the crisply baked
almond paste and remove that tiny slip
of white paper – flatten it, smooth it –
yearning to see printed there the words
of a gypsy, a voodoo witch – letters
rising faintly from burning incense
words shimmering inside flamelit crystal.
You want to be told what will happen, yes; you do
not want to be told what will happen, no. Both.

Announcements from the Planetarium *(mixtape #5)*

Astronomers can see the glow –
infrared radiation from dust
warmed by all the stars
burning since everything ever.

For right now though –
just give me one thing
I can hold on to, to believe
in this living is a hard way to go.

        Oh, you should keep on
        no matter how difficult –
        unless it kills you. Then
        you know you've gone too far.

...... including words from Kim A. McDonald / John Prine / Alice Neel

Roll over, Beethoven

*This is rock and roll. We should not be conservative
and we should not be safe.* ~ Cyndi Lauper

What if I set up a sound track of my life
on the *i*Pod, choosing a song, a theme
for every crucial scene, notable speech, realization?

For the moment I knew I could leave my marriage
is "Night on Bald Mountain" too obvious?

For clichés of bad faith adult behavior (example:
affair with married father of young children),
maybe something strident from *Carmen*?

Or should it all be doo-wop, R&B, rockabilly?
Because every song I heard in high school lives
inside my body. Inside, maybe, every cell.

'55-'56: Transistor radios! You could carry
the music! You could take it to the beach!

Even now, when memory bites us all, every note
every word is instantly available, total recall
shooting through me like adrenaline:

Bo Diddley/Fats Domino/Etta James/Elvis
– and Brenda Lee, who was younger than me.

I don't have those clothes anymore, but if I did –
I'd put them on and dance all night in Mickey's basement.

No doughnut

You don't happen to have a doughnut with you – do you?
No. I don't. But here's what I do have, that I could give you:

huge red cows standing
on the bare branches of a tree by the ocean
they look sad, they are quiet

fish so tiny they flicker like candles
in the darkest deep blue water

the raw cry of a big black bird
over and over in your ears with wind

mystery dust that must be from stars
at the farthest part of the universe
where scientists see they were wrong about everything

and a little slip of paper from a Chinese cookie that says
Among the lucky, you're the chosen one.

Speculative Music Theory:
   Like Dancing About Architecture #2

The course is called Early Music –
your professor talks at length
about a carillon, a remote Russian
chapel, years in the making.

But there were bells on the hood
of the baby carriage, tiny bells
that twinkled tiny tunes while
your mother pushed – you were
bundled inside, in blankets –
along the sidewalks of Cleveland
wrapped, rapt.

There was a bell on your tricycle
handlebars. Beside your bed
were drums the size elves play –
those were early too, miniature
jangling, booming – on the album
of the memory concert, music
you've been hearing all your life.

Sometimes the audience leaves the hall
to listen instead to YoYo Ma, or Billie
Holiday. Sometimes you leave too –
taking your coat. You'll be back.

Light falling here

(always, writers say, the light on the water
shines like diamonds, shines like gold
but the truth is that gold, and that diamonds
want only to shine like the light on the water)

Just now, on the early morning river
every spangle is a bird
flashing tiny wings of light;
the sun has thrown a sheet of hammered gold
over the slow skin of the dawn river;
a raft of light turns on dark water
tethered to the boat dock
moving with the river.

And I, waking here,
dreamed the sun falling down in the ocean
light in the heart of the sea
fire at the heart of the sea
my heart is on fire in the water
light burns in the heart of the sea
seawater skin on the body of sunset
sunset a fire at the watery edge of the world
fire all there at the edge of the world
burning the skin of the water
wet sand a mirror for fire in the water
sunset a tipped bowl of flame
I ask myself, again

Can I be in love with the light on the water? so in love that
I long for that light on the top of a mountain
and on the prairie need to touch it with my eyes?
In forest the light comes pouring all down, gilding a pool
where sun finds a break in the trees and I, mouth open
lips burning, kneel blinded inside the blaze.
I yearn for the liquid full moon, running silk silver all night
crave lightning on through the wash of the rain
weep at stars that tip waves in the lake.
I want to see fireclouds up in the sky
their waterhearts pierced by the sun
to drown through geometry gleaming in light
on the floor of a sunstruck pond.

Now again sun falls into ocean, moon rises out in far sky
they stream to me, here on the shore
light shivers the water, goldsilver crosses the sky
crosses the world, this whole world coming to me
the shivering glimmering path leads to me
just here to my face, to my feet
moons and suns rising and falling in water
light falling here into love.

Midrash on falling

August's intensity fools us in the city.
No one thinks about what's coming
until summer's long light falls
inside its own short night.

Children sing, run 'til they fall
split their skin like sweet tomatoes
bleed young juice, produce scars
they won't recognize in March
when blooms fall off camellias
or May when cherry blossoms fall
into plum apple peach petals drifting
across the early grass like December
snow falling over all who fall
into a dream   from grace   in love   away
falling like rain out of the air, falling
onto the singing children. All fall down.

Lois in the time available

In the time they said she had available, what
could be done? Not much, she was sure of that.
Nothing could be done, really, and she knew it.

Well, maybe something? No. Not much, she said
to herself again, and what she really meant was
nothing; that's what she meant by *not much.*

In more time, she thought, she could have done
something, made something, made something
happen. But there wasn't going to be more time.

There wasn't even time to improve something
already begun, or think again about something noted
(not begun yet, only noted) – for future use.

This, she could see now, was not going to be that
future. This was going to be another future – shorter:
a fragment of time, not what she would call useful.

If I were Zen, she thought, bits of time like this
would be no problem; they'd be opportunities.
I would use them to merge with the rain.

As it was, not Zen, she thought the time available
must be a waste. Then she wondered, could that be?
Is time truly *wasted?* Unused, laid aside, cast off?

Time, she thought, is simply an idea, invented
to make trains and breakfast easy for us to arrange.
So then it couldn't be wasted – could it?

Thinking this, she didn't regret those days, resent
or reject them (the few she'd be able to use), suddenly
knowing they would be the only time available.

White-Haired Women Would Dance for Us

In my country, when I was a girl
it was different. Yes, it was different
in my country, when I was a girl.

Now, there is like here. My sisters
tell me this happens, since the farms died.
My sisters tell me this happens: the farms
have died, and there is like here, now.

My country has water. Your soldiers drank
that water and left poison in the ground. Soon
we could not drink from our well. Poison
was there. This country has water. Soldiers
have come back. Now they are here, drinking.

There, then, the grandmothers could tell us
what to do. We would ask them to dream for us.
They always knew the past; they knew the future.
Our grandmothers knew the past and future
there, they could tell us what to do, there. When
we asked them to dream for us, they would tell us.

There, then, the white-haired grandmothers danced.
They would move like the corn, like wildflowers.
The white-haired women would sing for us then.
When we sang for them to dance, the white-haired
women would dance for all of us. The grandmothers
could move like flowers; they moved like cornsilk.
They danced to tell us how to be, tell us what to be.

When we came here, they would not come. We sang begging songs, pleading songs. We wanted them here with us. We tried to bring them here, with us. They said they should not come, dancing slowly beside the wells. They danced how they could not live outside that land. They said they would die if they came here. Oh! So much we wanted them, wanted to bring them with us, here. When we came here, the grandmothers would not come.

The American Dream

My people believed education
was the way, the truth, and the light.
They talked in a few languages
argued to help themselves think, and played cards for fun.

They were dark-haired people –
rich brown and shining black
hair that mostly fell into waves
sometimes had curls, and always caught the light like rivers do.

They kept celebrating religious
holidays after they didn't believe
in their god anymore. They did it
for pleasure: candlelight, music, food, sitting late at the table.

They climbed the class ladder –
fell down several rungs, climbed
up again, slid back down slowly.
Some of them, old, were able to die in Florida, in sunlight.

Wild river sister

Her bright hair is shining
flying over her mind
flying like river spray
like the white haired river –
green-blue water body
startling as turquoise
stones from the desert
gone loose, filled with light
running liquid, rushing
west over the land, west
to this cold water, thrashing
its white hair, racing
its own foam down a chute
between rocks – the river is
churning, like her mind.

Tom always asks the visiting poets about their influences;
this time, it's nature poets.

I did see what might have been
a kind of kingfisher, dark blue
perched in a white March aspen
tufted head displayed in profile.
Mary Oliver was nowhere nearby.
When my sharp intake of breath
– my surprise and tiny awe –
startled the bird into flight
I thought of her, the ways
into my urban mind she had
opened, years ago. I thought
of her prayers, her questions
and of my own.

Walking the woods in deep snow
I gave myself to quiet, readily
as I'd ever given myself (not
surrender, gift). Frost's poem
– the one with the little horse –
learned when I was fifteen
given to me though he didn't
mean to, was in my mind. His
words had taken me to trees
in the snow back then, so
trees in the snow took me back
to those words. No birds.
Flown south by now.

After a long life, the short version

Let me tell you about my childhood, how it was spent reading
Shakespeare as soon as I could slide a chubby finger across the
page of a faux folio, smudging the cheap ink.

Then I'll tell you about my adolescence, the time I refused
to speak for nineteen days and a counselor told my mother's
new husband I should be sent away with Rosenkrantz and
Guildenstern (or maybe it was Rosenberg and Greenglass).

Then I'll tell you about my years on the stage, my time as a
traveling player, those hot months of summer stock in the
southern states where the only respite, rare and thrilling, was
exiting the striped tent in the mowed field to sudden rain with
hail the size of olives, cherries, plum tomatoes.

Later I can talk about the marriages, the children, the group
therapy, the twelve step meetings and my days in the Safeway
parking lot collecting carts because I needed a job that didn't
require thinking. The pirate ship, the paper bag factory in
Copenhagen, the loading dock in East Timor – each promised
but did not deliver a do-not-think situation.

Finally, wandering the North American west, crossing and
recrossing rivers too fast and cold to soothe me, I won a door
prize at a Friday night square dance at the Elks Hall in Boise:
ten days, free, at a health club. Well! I wanted health, so I went.

Now all I want is the hot tub, want only to be submerged, to walk naked down white tile steps into nearly boiling water, to sit on the underwater ledge while fierce streams push hard against my spine. I don't care about the free weights, though I'm glad they've been liberated. I don't want to spin, except maybe straw into gold. I won't use the track, the tennis court, the machines – I want only that ritual bath, the cool shiver after, the shiny hair dryers, the little bowl of q-tips next to the stack of towels. The mirrored wall that tells me who I am.

THREE

You start out with one thing, end
up with another, and nothing's
like it used to be, not even the future.

- Rita Dove

"... but you may call me Maude."

...... in memoriam – Colin Higgins

Maude came to me in a dream. Really.
She was sitting at the kitchen table.
She was steeping a small pot of oatstraw
tea and had baked a little ginger pie
in my toaster oven. She came (she told
me) because she heard me say I wish
her hair had been white in the movie –
like it was, you know, in the book.

She said: Oh, but think – just think
about those people out in Hollywood.
It was rough – a struggle every day.
And Ruth looked good, didn't she?
Even with those bronze-brown braids
she never – not for one single minute
looked *young*! Everybody could see her
real skin – you can bet *that* was a battle!

I asked if she'd use bigger numbers
now, since people are living longer.
Then, she'd riffed on it: "I'll be eighty
next week / good time to move on /
seventy-five is too early / eighty-five
you're just marking time" – all that.
So, now, I asked her, how about maybe
ninety? Ninety-five? I wanted to know.

Truth is, she said to me, there should be
no numbers. Numbers are generic. Like
the daisy scene, when Ruth shows Bud
each flower is unique? Numbers aren't
really useful. Everybody's got to decide:
think about what's going on inside you –
body, mind – and outside too, the world!
Look at it all. That's how you know when.

The old woman gives advice *(mixtape #7)*

It takes a lot to laugh – it takes a train to cry.

Even so, it's never too late
to be what you might have been.

There is still time to do good things.
I'll help you but you must do just as I say.
Otherwise you'll get into trouble.

Here's the rule: Life is like riding a bicycle;
to keep your balance you must keep moving.

...... including words from Bob Dylan / MaryAnne Evans (called George Eliot) /
whoever put up the sign just north of Casita #2 on Los Panditos Road at the
Wurlitzer Foundation in Taos, New Mexico / Irene Tamony / Albert Einstein

Rapunzel, much later

I'm having an affair with my hair, seduced
by silver flashing white in the sun, brushing
the nape's lush secret – dark as it ever was.

Tendrils slide out of combs. Strands loosen
to fly in the wind, shining like the flash inside
my skull – lightning, streaking down to earth.

JohnPaulGeorge&Ringo Thought About It

Now we know the answer
to the Beatles' questions –
asked when I was not yet
thirty (but wondering).

Will you still need me
Will you still feed me
when I'm 64? Turns out –
some will, some won't.

Speculative Music Theory:
Like Dancing About Architecture #4

There's a man, a small man who's not young, who comes to play his trumpet at the farmers market. He's a dreadful musician, though this year is better than last; last year he played only "Happy Birthday" – over and over. This year he's playing a song that has two distinct lyric passages. He plays it repeatedly, pausing to say Good Morning in heavily accented English to people walking briskly to escape him. Fleeing shoppers walk away from the absurdly precious cookie stand and the fiercely serious farmer who grinds organic grains, toward the friendly women who tear the ferny tops off their bunches of carrots. The small man has his trumpet case open on the ground beside him, displaying his need for money. When people pass, rapidly, their faces are theater, masks of pity and shame inflected by pain from the awful noise. Sometimes they drop money in the case, suggesting that pity and shame may be stronger than pain.

Ferocious old women after work *(mixtape #4)*

I love my past.
I love my present.
I'm not ashamed
of what I've had
and I'm not sad
to have it no longer.

I always learned
what I needed to know.

My life extends over
a spectrum of history.

Here's what some think:
When you start out
it's about passions.
At the end it's intellectual.
Do you think that? I can't
even imagine it.

...... *including words from Colette / Frances Jaffer / Thomas E. Kennedy /*
Jean-Claude Ellena

Poem with things in every line

Start out with one thing
think of something
the thing you think you cannot do
the beautiful, needful thing

Remember everything
everything is fresh and glistening and firm
everything matters, though
everything we know is provisional

Slow things down
notice things that happen in this world
anything can happen
anything will happen

Things are not so bad now
things could be worse, though
nothing's like it used to be, when
nothing came between us and our lives

The elders repeat themselves

The condition of youth
is ignorance: they cannot
learn from us; they have to
bleed and gasp and weep.
Why tell them anything?

Why clutch their shoulders
pierce their eyes with ours
to fiercely whisper
all the burning years
into their open faces?

Given what we know, how can we
tell them what we say is true?

Tom Waits says the world keeps turning

– and I think about the Ferris wheel glowing
green yellow orange electric pink neon
slow circles of children shouting
grownups smiling while the carousel organ
grinds its heart out.

All the trees are listening. Music
is turning through light at the fair
and even though I know he means
something else, I have to ask with Tom –
How can anyone believe it all?

Metamorphoses

I may have become the old woman
    who lives in a cottage deep in the woods.

I might be the wolf who meets a child coming to visit
    carrying her basket of bread and jam for Granny.

Perhaps I'm a wicked stepmother urging her man to abandon
    his children – or the shallow, careless father who does.

I could be one of the thickly branching oaks, a rough pebble
    among their roots – a mossy stone, or a beetle climbing over it.

What if I were an ivory owl, swooping at those cheeky squirrels
    taking one while the others scatter in terror of my wings?

No reason not to be a fox, clever and plush, or a mushroom
    rising silently out of the dense bracken.

Even the dark bird who watches from the top of the tall aspen
    when children leave home wearing mittens and scarves.

I see those children waiting for the yellow bus.
    They have no idea.

Know this *(mixtape #1)*

The old woman is dismantling herself.
Beneath her shaggy eyebrows, her eyes
peer out like bits of hard shiny black lava.

She says, Now honey, you put me down
easy. You know ah'm a cracked plate.
My titanium and plastic hip glows
on the x-ray screen. What I am
forgetting doubles every day.

　　　　Know this: We must embrace pain
　　　　and burn it as fuel for our journey.

...... including words from Alice Ryerson Hayes / Helen L. Berkey / Zora Neale Hurston /
Sondra Zeidenstein / Lucille Clifton / Kenji Miyazawa

Are we there yet?

Once I was a baby.
Twice I was a child.
Three times I grew up
thinking, Ah, this is it.
I'm forty! I'm fifty! Sixty!
This, this is the number.
I'm all grown up, this
is the grown up thing:
maturity, wisdom, all
they keep talking about –
I've gotten to it now.

But life kept on as before
so I could see I wasn't
there yet, there'd be more:
more to learn, to know
to understand and do.
When would I uncover
the secrets? Seventy?
Surely that'd be old –
really old, right? Even
if it's only the first gate
rusted, and creaking open.

FOUR

This life in the fire, I love it.
I want it,
this life.

- Linda Hogan

The word on the street

Turns out – they all say – seventy-five
to ninety is full of news, and the decade
up to Centuryville can be amazing.

I'm not going to pretend I don't think so.
Old as everybody's getting to be these days
that information's surely worth an extra nod.

Looks like we're going back to Methuselah
(in zippier nations anyway, the super-nations)
speeding backward, global warming flooring it

to the Stone Age. On the corner, word is we're
all getting seriously old again – just when it might
be wiser to settle for *nasty, brutish and short.*

The old woman is angry (again)

because (again) her actual self has been
denied – with a smile (of course), denial
offered as a favor, a kindness, a sweetness –
the speaker assuming she'll be flattered
to hear that who she is, the old woman
what she is, an old woman, is not really
(not now, not here) who or what she is.

"Oh no! Not even close!" says the cashier
when the old woman asks for the elder
discount on her grocery bill. The cashier
smiles as those words slap the old woman
sliding her credit card along the sensitive
rim of the register computer that will
(or will not) approve of her.

They always smile when they do this.
She can see what they expect: she will
accept denial, take erasure as the gift
they mean it to be. They're giving her
a gift, saving her from the awfulness
of her own true life, and they want her
to smile about it, join up and pretend
(makeup, hair dye, cosmetic surgery)
– pretend she's not who she really is:
a woman, grown old, out in the world
buying radishes, cereal, soap, cookies.

The woman who hands you a gun

Don't think because I'm old
I'm not learning anymore. No.
That's not how it goes. Right
now I'm on my way, leaving
town to be a carny, a barker
at the tattooed lady's tent flap
or the woman who hands you a gun
at the shooting gallery or hoops
to toss over baby dolls. It's got
to be something I don't have
to study or practice, something
I can slip right into, on-the-job
training. Because I don't have
that kind of time anymore.
I'm saying I'll be an intern
an apprentice – not a student.
I don't have time for that.

A disagreement among friends sitting in the park on a bench in the sun

One says the hardest part
about being old is admitting
to yourself you actually are.

But it's not hard for my old woman.
She loves saying it: I'm old now!
She says this to herself, and she
says it to everybody else too.

One says maybe the hardest
thing about it – being old – is
remembering when you were young.

But my old woman loves her young
memory, and before she was born, too:
history! Even the future: triumph of hope
or tragedy. She wants to love the future.

Neurologists now define memory as a creative process

This is the story of how we begin to remember. ~ Paul Simon

Now we know: memories are made like dreams –
asleep and awake, we are memory artists
rummaging through metaphoric tubes of paint
musical notes, photos and phrases and fabric –
art supplies scattered around the messy studios
of our selves.
              Every one of us is composing –
drafting, framing, making images and emotions
into what we can believe, a story we will tell
ourselves and everyone else – the story we will
say *happened.* The form and method are classical –
holding the fabled mirror up to life, we're seeking
meaning, clarity, coherence: verisimilitude.

So, is forgetting a refusal to create, a rejection
of composition – closing up and shutting down
the studio? What about old people? Maybe old
people forget because we're bored – all those years
same damn methods, same forms.
                        Enough realism!
We want to range farther out – magic and puzzles.
Abstraction, not logic. We're all into improv:
riffing, scatting, spinning mixtapes – whatever.
Silliness is seriously appealing. Seriously. We do
not want to make memory the old way. We reject
that assignment, set it aside. We're giving it over
to the young ones – just as it was given to us.

She flies with her own wings *(mixtape #6)*

Long ago there was a cheerful old woman living
alone in a small house halfway up a steep hill.
She had a few chickens and a pig, but very little else.
Her cheeks were red and looked over-ripe
for she now disdained the use of powder.
A healthy old woman with sagging cheeks
and a double chin, well able to carry her burden
of flesh, freed from restraining stays.

She might have said, like her spirit brother
Some people try to turn back their odometers.
Not me. I want people to know why I look like this.
I traveled a long way and some of the roads weren't paved.

...... including Oregon's state motto + words from Ethel Johnston Phelps / Colette /
Will Rogers

Game on

Let's change that old game
now that everything's
getting different. That one
you played in the car
when you were little, when
your dad drove across
Tennessee to Grandma's
house for Thanksgiving.
You probably remember it.

Let's do it this way now:
Animal / Virtual / Mutual
See? It can be all about us –
bionic as we are now
isolates wired together
inside an imaginary cloud –
hooked up, but unreal.
You can see already how
much fun it's going to be.

Twenty more Julys, if you're lucky *(mixtape #2)*

Hurry up please, it's time.

During these brief days
that you have strength
be quick, and spare
no effort of your wings.

Fifty years   parents
children   lovers
have walked with me
eating me like cake.

      This life in the fire, I love it.
      I want it,
      this life.

...... including words from Sondra Zeidenstein / TS Eliot – and publicans all over Britain / Jalal ad-Din Muhammad Balkhi (called Rumi) / Lucille Clifton / Linda Hogan

En la clase de español: significación y los verbos

En la clase de español, it's different. I own my life:
tengo setenta años. I have seventy years. And this
ownership goes beyond English: *en inglés* I say I am
seventy. *Simplemente*, I am those years. Those years
are me. And this is fine, *está bien*, however simple
the talking. But in translation, moving one to another,
not all the movement is simple. In both Americas, *los dos*
daily life contains the sublime. And Spanish names it.

When I pull on two shirts, a hat and a jacket, that's
because *hace frío*. A nameless power is pulling air
across the sky in waves, turning green leaves brown
paralyzing water – making cold, making cold happen.
If I were to say all that in my own words, as in court
where that's what they want, I'd have to swear I couldn't.
Porque en español, hace frío: it makes cold. But if you're
talking English, it's cold; it's just cold. Nothing happens.

As it happens, *hay mas;* there's more to consider. As when
for example, *tengo miedo,* I have fear. I'm not then simply
afraid, as I might be in words I was born to – no, no – *en
la clase de español,* I have fear. I own it. Fear is my own.
And *en clase también*, also in Spanish class, *tengo hambre*:
I have hunger. I own the hunger inside of me, *sí*. I hold it
inside like the fear, *hambre como miedo*. They are mine.
Tengo los dos: el hambre y el miedo. Both belong to me.

On a clear night you can see the dark

Aged women are deepening inside
that visible darkness, shining like black
water in a forest pool, silver shaded
beneath branches tangling above, falling
breaking the shadowed mirror surface.

The crone, our mother, she who on earth
is a mountain, a tree, a cave with eyes of fire
a fierce mare bending her great neck to drink –
we feel her lips sliding along our softening
skin like a kiss as we pass through the moon.

Out here in the bigger numbers

Today when I was brushing my teeth
I noticed my eyebrows are different
from what they used to be (brown, dark).
As an entry-level old person, naturally
I'd seen a few light hairs a while back.
This is one of the suddenly-seen changes:
now both brows are tweed, variegated –
an attractive effect, definitely. I like it.

Unlikely to get me put on a watchlist
(as slow-growing cataracts have done)
my eyebrows' elegant silvering is one
of those lovely bits we find out here
in the bigger numbers – like the value
of gathering knowledge, loving years
of long friendship, the shock of creative
memory, the shy rise of hope against history.

You never think it's not what you want

We know it's wise to chew our food slowly
though long ago, in the wild – and also now
at the drive-through, this hasn't always been
possible (so much that's wise seems, so often
not possible)

Long ago and far away, early in the species
chewing slowly was a luxury or something
for herbivores – the cud groups, not our zippy
primate team of cousins; chewing slowly could
be dangerous

On holidays though, a slow chew might save you
from predators across the table: long-toothed
in-laws, former lovers, crazy neighbors, your
own grown children – the typical assortment
in December

That month of longest night and shortest light
has way too many holidays – food is featured
every time: served at tables, handed 'round
on small trays, displayed for grazing guests
who say yes, yes

December food is like toys, like giftwrap, like
decoration – admired for its design, shining
in the glitter of sparkling lights that dramatize
the clever art of its frosting, its stuffing or shape
(unnatural)

So well prepared is all that food, so generously
portioned and carefully contrived for delight
you never think it's not what you want – won't
be what you can use, won't be what you need
after the ball

When the party's over, the new year rung in (you
really *did* get there with bells on) your calendar
looks just like last year – the months named
January and so on; the weeks, again, all start with
Monday, Tuesday

You dared to hope for something, you had some
expectations, you made plans, you even thought
the earth was your model, turning toward the light
but you forgot it never stops – all of forever just
keeps on turning

...... for Nicole

No matter what's happening,

in the middle of whatever you must be doing
stop to think about stars
wildly far away, burning up there so long
and
think about the heat of connection
between you and everything
how that heat moves
sometimes thumping like a slightly broken motor
the kind with a rotating drum
and
think about how everything sometimes
gets sticky, like candy in a valentine box left in the sun
on the back porch, balanced on the railing's corner
where the floorboards are warped, tipping
just enough to make you dizzy
while you stand there
looking up.

...... for Gwyn

About the Author

Born and raised in the Great Lakes region, Judith Arcana has lived in the Pacific Northwest since 1995. She writes poems, stories, essays and books, including a well-loved biography of Grace Paley (*Grace Paley's Life Stories*) and the poetry collections *What if your mother*, *4th Period English*, *The Parachute Jump Effect*, and *Here From Somewhere Else*, which received the Editor's Choice Chapbook Award from *Turtle Island Quarterly*. Her story *Soon To Be A Major Motion Picture* won the first Minerva Rising Prose Prize and was published as a chapbook; *Keesha and Joanie and JANE*, her zine about what happens when Roe v Wade is overturned in the near future, is rooted in her work as a Jane in Chicago's underground abortion service (Judith has written a collection of JANE stories and hopes they'll be a book someday). She hosts a monthly poetry show on KBOO community radio in Oregon (listen online anywhere/anytime). For more about – and examples of – her work, visit JudithArcana.com.

Acknowledgements / Gratitude

The following poems first appeared (some in earlier versions and/or with different titles) in these publications: Fullerton - *5AM*; Light, falling here - *Nimrod*; What the birds say - *Poems and Plays*; No doughnut - *Poetry East*; The crows - *Junctures*; The woman who hands you a gun - *Cirque*; The first true thing - *Manzanita Quarterly*; You may have heard - *Persimmon Tree*; Roll Over, Beethoven - *Ghost Town Poetry*, V2; You Never Think It's Not What You Want - *The Parachute Jump Effect*; Lois in the time - *Passager*; En la clase - *Red Cedar Review*; Midrash - *Bridges*; Nickel Heart + The Sun in Montana - *Diner*; After a Long Life + Are we there yet + Wild river sister + White-Haired Women + Writings in SMT #1, 2, 3 - *Elohi Gadugi*; Almost Never - *Thresholds*; The elders repeat themselves - *Umbrella*; The god of your body - *you say. say.*; Zombies on Skateboards - *Calyx*; Metamorphoses + Dreaming the Indian Ocean - *Here From Somewhere Else*; On a clear night - *Whale Road Review*; The old woman is angry - **82 review*; 1956 - *Cimarron Review*; Tom always asks the visiting poets - *Turtle Island Quarterly*.

I'm grateful for grants from NW Oregon's Regional Arts and Culture Council and Portland's Celebration Foundation, both of which supported the writing of many of these poems. I'm grateful to Sondra Zeidenstein and Penelope Scambly Schott, who read some of these poems in early draft versions; to Constance Hall and Steve Williams for sparking one line in "Zombies on Skateboards"; to Ann Skvarek and Jason Fayen for generous hospitality; to David Bogue for connection; to Michael Spring and Ryan Forsythe for skill and goodness. I'm thankful for the work – and attitude – of the late Alice Neel, who painted a nude self-portrait when she was 75. I'm thankful to Jonathan Arlook, always.

Also by Judith Arcana

Here From Somewhere Else
Soon To Be A Major Motion Picture
Keesha and Joanie and JANE
The Parachute Jump Effect
4th Period English
What if your mother
Grace Paley's Life Stories, A Literary Biography
Every Mother's Son
Our Mothers' Daughters

www.ingramcontent.com/pod-product-compliance
Lightning Source LLC
Chambersburg PA
CBHW071354090426
42738CB00012B/3120